The Wisdom of
Old-Time Baseball

The Wisdom of Old-Time Baseball

Common Sense and Uncommon Genius
From 101 Baseball Greats

Compiled and Edited by Criswell Freeman

WALNUT GROVE PRESS
Nashville, TN
(615) 256-8584

ISBN 1-887655-08-5

The ideas expressed in this book are not, in all cases, exact quotations, as some have been edited for clarity and brevity. In all cases, the author has attempted to maintain the speaker's original intent. In some cases, material for this book was obtained from secondary sources, primarily print media. While every effort was made to ensure the accuracy of these sources, the accuracy cannot be guaranteed. For additions, deletions, corrections or clarifications in future editions of this text, please write WALNUT GROVE PRESS.

Printed in the United States of America

Book Design by Armour&Armour
Cover Design by Mary Mazer
Typesetting & Page Layout by Sue Gerdes
Edited by Alan Ross and Angela Beasley
1 2 3 4 5 6 7 8 9 10 • 96 97 98 99 00 01

For David Talley

Great Coach – Even Greater Friend

Table of Contents

Introduction 13

Chapter 1: The Game 15

Chapter 2: All-Purpose Advice 23

Chapter 3: Life 35

Chapter 4: The Mental Game 43

Chapter 5: Hard Work 51

Chapter 6: Adversity 59

Chapter 7: Success 69

Chapter 8: The Great Ones 77

Chapter 9: Great Moments 91

Chapter 10: Hitting 97

Chapter 11: Pitching 107

Chapter 12: Playing the Field 119

Chapter 13: Managing 127

Chapter 14: Winning and Losing 135

Chapter 15: Observations 143

Sources 157

Introduction

Baseball, more than any other sport, connects us to our memories. As we reminisce about Willie or The Mick or Stan or Hammerin' Hank, we are transported to a simpler time. It is a time of transistor radios and sliding pads. We recall the smell of freshly cut grass and the crack of a well-hit ball. We can hear the voices of our favorite announcers, and we can see the classic swings of the game's unforgettable sluggers. Baseball memories don't just live in our minds, they also live in our hearts.

This book chronicles wisdom and humor from 101 of baseball's greatest legends; it also includes quotations from other notable characters, including writers, announcers and owners. I have chosen 1969 — the year of The Miracle Mets — as the cutoff date. Players whose careers began after that magic year are, at least for me, newcomers; they must wait a few decades for their tribute.

The old-timers in this book embody the joy, the elegance and the common-sense genius of America's pastime. Their insights spring from decades of hard work and struggle. Some, like Branch Rickey and Jackie Robinson, are more than baseball heroes, they are American heroes. Others, like Mickey Mantle, have earned more than our admiration — they have earned our affection. Still others, like The Babe, are as much a part of American history as the War of 1812.

Share the wisdom of the game's greatest legends, and while you're at it, take a side trip down memory lane. You'll discover a secret that lies hidden inside the faded leather of your childhood fielder's mitt: When it comes to baseball memories, the laws of time and space simply don't apply.

1

The Game

In 1879, The Cincinnati Gazette proclaimed, "The baseball mania has run its course. It has no future as a professional endeavor." This prediction brings to mind the words of Pete Rose, who said, "Half the stuff you read in the papers isn't true, but what can you expect for thirty-five cents?"

The following quotations extol the virtues of a game that has entertained Americans for 150 years. We play the game; we observe the game; we discuss the game. And we cherish memories of seasons and heroes past.

How long will baseball endure? Brooks Robinson once observed, "I wouldn't mind playing baseball forever." The rest of us, it seems, wouldn't mind watching.

The only real game in the world, I think,
          is baseball.

Babe Ruth

If we in America have a national game,
          it is baseball.

A. G. Spalding

Baseball is in its infancy.

Charles H. Ebbets, 1913

No matter what I talk about, I always
          get back to baseball.

Connie Mack

There is nothing now heard of in our
          leisure hours except ball, ball, ball.

Henry Wadsworth Longfellow

Next to religion, baseball has furnished
a greater impact on American life
than any other institution.

Herbert Hoover

Every boy builds a shrine to some baseball
hero, and before that shrine
a candle always burns.

Judge Kenesaw Mountain Landis

The day Custer lost at the Little Bighorn,
the Chicago White Sox beat the Cincinnati
Red Legs, 3–2. Both teams wore knickers,
and they are still wearing them today.

Charlie Finley

Ninety feet between bases is perhaps
as close as man has ever gotten to perfection.

Red Smith

The game of ball is glorious.

Walt Whitman

Baseball is an island of surety
in a changing world.

Bill Veeck

Baseball is continuity: pitch to pitch,
inning to inning, game to game,
series to series, season to season.

Ernie Harwell

Baseball has a funny way
of giving us treasured memories.

Brooks Robinson

Baseball's unique possession is
the fan's memory of the times
his daddy took him to the game to see
the great players of his youth.

Bill Veeck

Baseball is a game that allows us
to stay young at heart.

Tommy John

When you watch baseball at its best,
there's a tendency to forget the real world.

Mickey Mantle

I'm 81, but I can feel like I'm 15
when I'm talking baseball.

Buck O'Neil

To play baseball, it's necessary only
to have a ball, a bat, a glove, and
the imagination of a young boy.

Branch Rickey

In baseball, you can't kill the clock.
You've got to give the other man his chance.
That's why this is the greatest game.

Earl Weaver

It's still the best game in town because you
don't have to be big to play, and everybody
plays. Even your grandmother
probably played baseball.

Tommy Lasorda

Baseball is a most orderly thing
in a very unorderly world. If you get
three strikes, even the best lawyer
in the world can't get you off.

Bill Veeck

Baseball is a game to be savored
rather than taken in gulps.

Bill Veeck

I have never known a day when I didn't learn
something new about the game.

Connie Mack

Baseball is like church.
Many attend, but few understand.

Wes Westrum

The saddest day of the year
is the day baseball season ends.

Tommy Lasorda

What a great day for baseball. Let's play two.

Ernie Banks

2

All-Purpose Advice

In 1665, La Rouchfoucauld wrote, "One gives nothing so freely as advice." The French philosopher could have been writing about baseball. From the Little Leagues to the big leagues, everyone, it seems, is a self-styled expert. Coaches and managers provide a constant stream of instruction while fans scream their own opinions. On the baseball diamond, advice is everywhere.

The game is played at a leisurely pace, with plenty of time to sit and talk. It's no surprise that baseball's greatest legends became do-it-yourself ballpark philosophers. Countless hours in the dugout provided ample opportunity to consider not only baseball, but also the human condition. Here's what they discovered ...

Never surrender opportunity to security.
> *Branch Rickey*

Keep your head up and
you may not have to keep it down.
> *Joe McCarthy*

Keep your alibis to yourself.
> *Christy Mathewson*

Don't try to be somebody you're not.
They tried to make me into the mold of Babe
Ruth, but I didn't want to fit anyone's mold.
> *Roger Maris*

Take time to thank everyone
who has helped you along the way.
Brooks Robinson

Study the game, accept advice, keep fit,
and above all, save your money.
Babe Ruth

Go lightly on the vices,
such as carrying on in society.
The social ramble ain't restful.
Satchel Paige

If you don't know where you're going,
be careful. You might get there.
Yogi Berra

Nobody ever said, "Work ball!"
They say, "Play ball!" To me,
that means having fun.

Willie Stargell

Be on time. Bust your butt. Play smart.
And have some laughs along the way.

Whitey Herzog

Generate happiness within yourself.

Ernie Banks

Play happy.

Willie Mays

Don't tell them what you did in the past;
tell them what you are going
to do in the future.

Stan Musial

If what you did yesterday still looks big to you,
you haven't done much today.

Chief Bender

Last year is past history. Never look back.
Go back out and beat 'em again this year.

Casey Stengel

Do your best and forget the rest.

Walter Alston

Don't look back.
Something might
be gaining on you.

Satchel Paige

Rule number one in my book reads,
    "Don't fight the umpires.
      It's bad business."
Babe Ruth

Don't beef at the umpire. Fury is hard
    on you physically and emotionally.
Herb Pennock

Do not fight too much with the umpires.
    You cannot expect them to be
      as perfect as you.
Joe McCarthy

Don't be afraid to take advice.
There's always something new to learn.

Babe Ruth

When you're through learning,
you're through.

Vernon Law

It's what you learn after you know it all
that counts.

Earl Weaver

If you can't imitate him, don't copy him.
Casey Stengel

Be patient – it's the most important thing.
Tris Speaker

You have to get your uniform dirty.
Pete Rose

All my life I tried to be honest with people.
I wish I had been a little more honest
with myself.
Mickey Mantle

Without hope, there is nothing.

Bob Gibson

Take care of your body. You only get one.

Mickey Mantle

Whatever you start, finish.

Mother's advice to Ferguson Jenkins

Keep hammering away.

Hank Aaron

If you come to a fork in the road, take it.

Yogi Berra

3
Life

Judge Kenesaw Mountain Landis observed, "Baseball is something more than a game to an American boy. It is his training field for life."

For over 150 years, baseball has helped teach us about adversity and courage, success and failure, disappointment and hope.

The following thoughts come courtesy of men who were well-trained in America's game — and in the game of life.

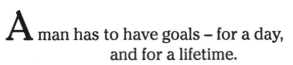

A man has to have goals – for a day,
and for a lifetime.

Ted Williams

You owe it to yourself to be the best
you can possibly be – in baseball
and in life.

Pete Rose

Every day is a new opportunity.
You can build on yesterday's success or put
its failures behind and start over. That's the
way life is, with a new game every day,
and that's the way baseball is.

Bob Feller

Take a swing at life. Now.

Mickey Mantle

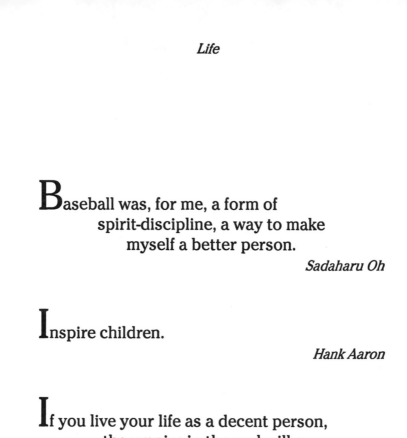

Baseball was, for me, a form of
spirit-discipline, a way to make
myself a better person.

Sadaharu Oh

Inspire children.

Hank Aaron

If you live your life as a decent person,
the umpire in the end will say
you did it right.

Harry Caray

A life isn't significant except for its impact on other lives.

Jackie Robinson

It's a mere moment in a man's life between
an All-Star game and an old-timer's game.

Vin Scully

Age is a question of mind over matter.
If you don't mind, it don't matter.

Satchel Paige

The trick is growing up without growing old.

Casey Stengel

The future isn't what it used to be.

Yogi Berra

There comes a time in every man's life,
and I've had plenty of them.

Casey Stengel

To live in harmony with your surroundings
is to be reminded that every end
is followed by a new beginning.

Sadaharu Oh

They say you have to be good to be lucky,
but I think you have to be lucky to be good.

Rico Carty

Some things in life you just can't buy –
like great memories.

Don Drysdale

4

The Mental Game

In baseball, performance is a function of attitude. Expect to strike out, and you will. Fear the curveball, and you'll never hit it. Rocky Colavito summed it up when he said, "There's only one way to make it in this game: Have confidence in yourself."

Success on the diamond has a way of snowballing. But if confidence wanes, watch out. Billy Williams understood the psychosomatic nature of baseball when he observed, "A slump starts in your head and ends up in your stomach."

Perhaps Yogi Berra said it best. "Baseball," he noted, "is ninety percent mental. The other half is physical." Enough said.

Worry is simply thinking the same thing
over and over again – and
not doing anything about it.

Branch Rickey

No man can have a "yellow streak" and last.
He must not pay much attention
to his nerves and temperament.

Christy Mathewson

You can't have a long, successful career
without a positive attitude.

Nolan Ryan

The difference between the possible
and the impossible lies in
a person's determination.

Tommy Lasorda

In order to have confidence,
you have to perform well.
Then confidence builds on itself.

Monte Irvin

My philosophy has always been simple:
Believe in yourself.

Tommy John

It's better to throw a theoretically poorer
pitch wholeheartedly, than to throw the
so-called right pitch with a feeling of doubt.

Sandy Koufax

Self-confidence is the hallmark
of a champion – any champion.

Grantland Rice

The guy who can control his emotions
on the field is the guy who's great.

Robin Roberts

A ballplayer who can't keep his cool
is worse than no ballplayer at all.

Lou Gehrig

Don't waste yourself being negative.
Go for the positive.

Ty Cobb

You gotta believe.

Tug McGraw

The greatest teacher is visualization.
You see others do it, and you aspire
to reach that level.

Tony Kubek

Prefer the errors of enthusiasm
to the complacency of wisdom

Branch Rickey

There's a good kind of ignorance.
Sometimes you're just too dumb to know
you can't do the impossible.

Joe Garagiola

You can't let any team awe you.

Luke Appling

Fear promotes failure.
Humor controls fear.

Tim McCarver

Show me a guy who's afraid to look bad,
and I'll show you a guy you can beat.

Lou Brock

If you're afraid, you'll never do the job.

Bill Mazeroski

Never let the fear
of striking out
get in your way.

Babe Ruth

Make optimism a way of life.

Brooks Robinson

5

Hard Work

Old-time ballplayers never enjoyed the silver spoon. In baseball's golden age, million-dollar contracts did not exist; neither did fat signing bonuses. Salaries were meager, so the off-season was a time for players to earn a few extra bucks.

Before he was called up to the majors, a promising young kid named Mantle took summer employment alongside has father, Mutt. Mickey recalled, "The year before I went to the Yankees, I worked in the mines with Dad. Nobody cared if I was a future Yankee star or the King of Siam." Today, a prospect with Mantle's skills would never work in a zinc mine, although he might own one.

Old-timers learned about work the hard way. On the following pages, they share a few lessons.

Dad always said,
  "Practice, practice, practice."
Dad was right. Practice paid off.
                    Mickey Mantle

Practice, work hard, and give it
          everything you have.
                    Dizzy Dean

Practice hard and long.
                    Babe Ruth

You can always take what you have
          and make it better.
                    Ted Williams

A good hitter does a little thinking,
  a little playing, and a lot of practicing.
                    Pete Rose

Work at what doesn't come easy to you.

Ty Cobb

A baseball swing is a finely tuned instrument.
It is repetition and more repetition
then a little more after that.

Reggie Jackson

By the sweat of thy brow shalt thou earn
thy bread. Labor and toil – and something else:
a joy in one's work.

Branch Rickey

The way is long and the mastery of any sort
is not easy to achieve.

Sadaharu Oh

Nobody can become a ballplayer
by walking after a ball.

Joe McCarthy

You'd be surprised how many shortcomings
you overcome by hustle.

Pete Rose

You've got to be lucky, but then you've got
to be able to take advantage of your luck.

Chuck Conners

Study and work at the game
as if it were a science.

Ty Cobb

An athlete needs God-given ability,
but discipline achieves success.

Ferguson Jenkins

Sweat is the greatest solvent for problems.

Branch Rickey

There is nothing owed to you.

Bill Veeck

If you can't outsmart people, outwork them.

Bill Veeck

Work is the zest of life.
There is joy in its pursuit.

Branch Rickey

I love baseball. It beats working.

Yogi Berra

I never had a job.
I always played baseball.

Satchel Paige

Luck is the residue of design.

Branch Rickey

6

Adversity

Baseball is built around adversity. The batter who fails seven times out of ten is an all-star. The team that wins sixty percent of its games takes the pennant. Clearly, the ball field is a place where character is put to the anvil.

In 1980, Reds outfielder Cesar Geronimo became Nolan Ryan's 3,000th strikeout victim. Ironically, he had been Bob Gibson's 3,000th strikeout in 1974. When questioned about this dubious coincidence, Geronimo shrugged off his adversity and replied, "I guess I was just in the right place at the right time." Hail Cesar!

Experience is
a tough teacher.
It gives the test before
presenting the lesson.

Vernon Law

Whether it's injury or personal tragedy,
survival rests on being able to prove yourself,
over and over again.

Tommy John

You never have to wait long, or look far,
to be reminded of how thin the line is
between being a hero or a goat.

Mickey Mantle

Some days you eat the bear,
and some days the bear eats you.

Preacher Roe

If the world was perfect, it wouldn't be.

Yogi Berra

Playing in the big league wasn't
    nearly as hard as getting there.

Hank Aaron

Pitchers did me a favor when they knocked
    me down. It made me more determined.

Frank Robinson

Everything good that has happened to me
has happened as a result of something bad.

Harry Caray

Tragedy offers you a different perspective
on life. There are far more important things
    than wins and losses.

Tommy John

Remembering the good times
    gets you through the bad times.

Walter Alston

They say it can't be done,
but that doesn't
always work.

Casey Stengel

Take the errors and breaks out of baseball,
and the game would die within a few weeks.
You play the best you know how, and if
you lose, you should have no regrets.
John McGraw

You can't be afraid to make errors.
No one ever masters baseball or conquers it.
You only challenge it.
Lou Brock

Look at misfortune the same way
you look at success. Don't panic.
Walter Alston

Problems are the price you pay for progress.
Branch Rickey

Do not alibi on bad hops.
Anybody can field
the good ones.

Joe McCarthy

There are bad days and good days,
bad months and good months, bad years and
good years. If you lose, pick yourself up and
carry on. That's baseball.
And that's life.

Tim McCarver

In baseball, there's always another game
tomorrow, and if not tomorrow, then the next
day. Some seasons you find yourself waiting
for a lot of tomorrows.

Walter Alston

In baseball, there's always tomorrow.
Maybe you got me today, but tomorrow,
I'm coming back.

Buck O'Neil

The best thing about
baseball is that you
can do something about
yesterday tomorrow.

Manny Trillo

It ain't over
till it's over.

Yogi Berra

7

Success

In Ty Cobb's day, baseball was not a gentleman's profession. The game was played by tough guys, hooligans and roughnecks, none of whom intimidated the pugnacious young Cobb.

When Ty told his father of his desire to turn pro, the elder Cobb warned, "Don't come home a failure." For better or for worse, those words rang in Ty's ears until the day he died.

Success is difficult to define. Cobb became one of the greatest hitters to ever swing a bat, but he so embittered his peers that at his funeral, only four baseball men attended.

Did Ty Cobb follow his father's advice? One must wonder.

Success doesn't just happen.
You've got to make it happen.

Joe McCarthy

Everything is possible to him who dares.

A. G. Spalding

Sweat plus sacrifice equals success.

Charlie Finley

The only problem with success is that
it doesn't teach you how
to deal with failure.

Tommy Lasorda

You'll never reach second base
　　if you keep one foot on first.

Vernon Law

Do a thing as well as it can be done.

Ty Cobb

A fellow doesn't last long
　　on what he's done. He's got to keep on
　　　　delivering as he goes along.

Carl Hubbell

A great baseball player is one
　　who will take a chance.

Branch Rickey

If you aren't happy in one place,
    chances are pretty good you won't be
        happy in another place.

Ernie Banks

Happiness is good friends
    and a good bull pen.

Bob Lemon

Enthusiasm has to be generated
    day in and day out. It's the only way
    to play winning baseball.

Earl Weaver

To be a major leaguer,
    you have to be a man, but you have
    to have a lot of boy in you, too.

Roy Campanella

Success is being truly happy at what you do.

Tommy Lasorda

Every player should have goals to keep his interest up. Goals should be realistic and they should reflect improvement.

Ted Williams

More men fail through lack of purpose than lack of talent.

Billy Sunday

If you have skills, it's easy to play the game. But it's what you do off the field that dictates whether or not you're a star.

Willie Mays

If you work hard every day and bust your butt on every play, people notice, and word gets around.

Tommy John

Aggressiveness plus enthusiasm
        equals hustle.

Pete Rose

Always run them out. You never can tell.

Joe McCarthy

The only way to make progress
        is to make more progress.

Branch Rickey

For when that One Great Scorer
        comes to mark against your name,
He writes – not that you won or lost –
        but how you played the game.

Grantland Rice

You just can't beat
the person who
never gives up.

Babe Ruth

8

The Great Ones

The Swiss psychiatrist Carl Jung observed, "Great talents are the loveliest fruits on the tree of humanity." So it is on the baseball diamond: Greatness is a joy to watch.

In his day, there was no better judge of talent than Branch Rickey. Rickey understood that a fine line separates greatness from mediocrity.

Mr. Rickey was once asked to name the best players he'd ever seen. He responded simply, "The great players of all time are the ones with zest."

For each generation, a few unforgettable players dominate center stage. On the following pages, we share a few words about men who played with zest. We remember them because greatness, once observed, is not forgotten.

Babe Ruth was the single greatest magnet
that sport has ever known.

Grantland Rice

I didn't room with Babe.
I roomed with his suitcase.

Ping Bodie

All the lies about Babe Ruth are true.

Waite Hoyt

The greatness of Ty Cobb was something
that had to be seen, and to see him
was to remember him forever.

George Sisler

The greatest hitter I ever saw was Ty Cobb.

Babe Ruth

Cobb and Ruth – they stand alone.

Ted Williams

Who are my Four Masters?
In no special order they are Cy Young,
Walter Johnson, Grover Alexander
and Christy Mathewson.

Grantland Rice

Matty was without a peer.
He had a greater variety of stuff than any
pitcher I ever knew. And he was one of the
finest sportsmen the game has ever known.

John McGraw

God was responsible for Walter Johnson.

Branch Rickey

Lou Gehrig was a man who came through
in the clutch above all others.

Joe McCarthy

I don't make speeches. I just let my bat
speak for me in the summertime.

Honus Wagner

A homer a day will boost your pay.

Josh Gibson

I played for Casey Stengel
before and after he was a genius.

Warren Spahn

Stan Musial had 3,630 hits:
    1,815 at home and 1,815 on the road.
       Talk about consistency.
Tim McCarver

You could make a study of Musial's life and
learn how to be a decent human being.
Branch Rickey

The best way to pitch Musial?
Walk him and try to pick him off first base.
Joe Garagiola

Stan Musial is living proof
    that nice guys don't finish last.
Ken Boyer

Ted Williams sees more of the ball
than any man alive.

Ty Cobb

Never pitch to Ted Williams in a close game
if there is a base open. Any base.

Bob Feller

Ted Williams was the greatest hitter
I ever saw.

Mickey Mantle

Before I was ever born, my dad had a name picked out. Mickey – after Mickey Cochrane, the great hitting catcher who spent his entire career in the American League.

Mickey Mantle

Mantle was as much a symbol of baseball as Cracker Jacks.

Bob Costas

Mickey Mantle, always so hard on himself, finally came to accept and appreciate the difference between a role model and a hero. The first he often was not. The second he will always be.

Bob Costas

Willie Mays was the best ballplayer
I ever saw. Period.

Tim McCarver

I believed that when I went on that field,
I was on stage.

Willie Mays

Who was better, me or Mays?
Over a full career, it was Willie.

Mickey Mantle

We kept an eye on each other,
Willie and me.

Mickey Mantle

Branch Rickey was a giant among Pygmies.

Red Smith

If a black man can make it
on Okinawa and Guadalcanal,
he can make it in baseball.

Happy Chandler

I'm looking for a ballplayer
with enough guts not to fight back.

Branch Rickey to Jackie Robinson

Baseball became an all-American sport
in 1947, and two people made it possible:
Mr. Branch Rickey and Mr. Bill Veeck.

Larry Doby

The more they rode Jackie Robinson,
the better he played.

Roy Campanella

I'm not concerned with being liked or disliked.
I'm concerned with being respected.

Jackie Robinson

Jackie Robinson was the greatest competitor
I ever saw.

Duke Snider

Jackie Robinson was Ty Cobb in technicolor.

Bill "Bojangles" Robinson

Satchel Paige threw the ball
as far from the bat and as close to the plate
as possible.

Casey Stengel

Satchel Paige did for black baseball
what Ruth did for white baseball.

Buck O'Neil

In his day, Bob Feller
was the best pitcher living.

Joe DiMaggio

If I had to choose one person to pitch one
game in my one lifetime,
I would choose Bob Gibson.

Curt Flood

Forget Walter Johnson. You can forget Waddell.
That Jewish kid Koufax is probably
the best of them all.

Casey Stengel

As far as I'm concerned, Joe DiMaggio
was probably the greatest all-around
baseball player who ever lived.

Mickey Mantle

Joe DiMaggio was the greatest ballplayer
of our time. He could do it all.

Ted Williams

Williams was the most natural hitter,
but Berra was the most natural ballplayer.

Casey Stengel

Ernie Banks was so popular that hitting him
with a pitch was like hitting the Pope.

Don Drysdale

Trying to sneak a pitch past Hank Aaron was
like trying to sneak the sunrise past a rooster.

Joe Adcock

Brooks Robinson is the best fielding
third baseman I've ever seen.

Pie Traynor

Brooks Robinson belongs
in a higher league.

Pete Rose

You couldn't believe Roberto Clemente
until you saw him play. And then,
you could never forget.

Earl Weaver

I want to be remembered as a ballplayer
who gave all he had to give.

Roberto Clemente

Pete Rose seemed to have an obligation to hit.

Lou Brock

9

Great Moments

Each spring, I burrow in my closet and bring out a glove that Dad gave me when I was ten. It is a Warren Spahn model, and it still does the job quite nicely. As I pitch with my daughter, that old glove reminds me of a profound truth: Time passes but memories remain.

Baseball is a game of memories. We cherish recollections of home runs hit and ball games won; we never totally forget the tough losses.

A handful of baseball memories are universally burned into the collected consciousness of fans everywhere. The following quotations memorialize great moments in baseball history. Remember and enjoy.

Lou Gehrig will not be in the lineup today.
Babe Dahlgren will take his place.

Joe McCarthy

For the past two weeks you've been hearing
about a bad break I got. But today
I consider myself the luckiest man
on the face of the earth.

Lou Gehrig

Yankee Stadium, July 4, 1939

I've often wondered how a man who knew
he was about to die could stand here and
say he was the luckiest man in the world.
But now I think I know how Lou Gehrig felt.

Mickey Mantle

The day his number was retired at Yankee Stadium

The Giants win the pennant!
The Giants win the pennant!
The Giants win the pennant!
They're going crazy – I don't believe it!
I don't believe it. I do not believe it!

Russ Hodges
Announcing Bobby Thomson's game-winning home run in the Giant's National League playoff win over the Dodgers, October 3, 1951

I didn't think home run.
I just wanted to hit it some place fair.

Bobby Thomson

I kept saying, "Sink, sink, sink,"
but I knew he couldn't catch it.
I remember thinking,
"Why me?"

Ralph Branca
After giving up Bobby Thomson's "shot heard around the world"

I'm glad it's over.
   Keltner was a little rough on me tonight.
                                    Joe DiMaggio
        After ending his 56-game hitting streak

My main aim was to win. It was just
   another loss, but it hurt a little more.
                                    Harvey Haddix
      After pitching 12 perfect innings and losing in the 13th

Nothing ever hurt as bad
   as Mazeroski's home run.
                                    Mickey Mantle

Say it ain't so, Joe.

*Young boy's comment, probably apocryphal,
to Shoeless Joe Jackson after the
Black Sox Scandal*

Last night I was a bum. Tonight everyone wants to meet me.

Don Larson

After his World Series perfect game

10

Hitting

Hitting is a mysterious skill. It requires quickness, strength, vision, courage and sound judgment, yet all of these, taken together, cannot guarantee greatness. What makes a Babe Ruth or a Henry Aaron? Man speculates, but only God can be certain.

Many have tried to unravel the riddle. Stan Musial said, "The secret of hitting is physical relaxation and mental concentration." The Man was right, to a point, but no less an expert than Ty Cobb admitted, "Batting is a problem you solve over and over again, but never master."

The following words of wisdom may raise your average, but be forewarned: When it comes to the weird science of hitting, there are no guarantees.

Hitting is 50% above the shoulders.

Ted Williams

Batting is more mental than physical.

Ty Cobb

Nothing will stop a hitter as quickly
as fear and tension at the plate.

Charlie Lau

The key to hitting is to relax, concentrate –
and don't hit the ball to center field.

Stan Musial

If you get fooled by a pitch
with less than two strikes, take it.

Ted Williams

Swing through the ball, not at it.
Visualize a line through the box.

Charlie Lau

You don't have to leave it all up to chance.
There are ways to prepare yourself by figuring
out what the pitcher's going to throw.

Ted Williams

Swing hard in case they throw the ball
where you're swinging.

Duke Snider

To be a good hitter, you've got to do one thing: Get a good ball to hit.

Rogers Hornsby

The art of hitting is getting your pitch.

Dr. Bobby Brown

You have to get good pitches to hit home runs.

Ted Williams

Don't swing at "almost strikes."

Babe Ruth

A hitter's impatience
  is the pitcher's biggest advantage.

Pete Rose

The pitcher has to throw a strike sooner or
later, so why not hit the pitch you want to hit
and not the one he wants you to hit?

Johnny Mize

A decent hitter can hit a good pitch
  three times better than a great hitter
    can hit a bad pitch.

Ted Williams

When you step into the batter's box,
have nothing on your mind except baseball.
Pete Rose

A full mind is an empty bat.
Branch Rickey

You can't think and hit at the same time.
Yogi Berra

Keep your eyes clear and hit 'em where they ain't.

Wee Willie Keeler

Every great hitter works on the theory
that the pitcher is more afraid of him
than he is of the pitcher.

Ty Cobb

I don't like to sound egotistical,
but every time I step up to the plate with a
bat in my hands, I feel sorry for the pitcher.

Rogers Hornsby

Fear strikes out.

Pete Rose

Get a strike and knock the heck out of it.

Stan Musial's hitting advice to Curt Flood

11

Pitching

In the early days of baseball, a pitcher's job was simple: lob the ball over the plate. Thankfully, that job description changed. Eventually, hurlers stopped throwing the ball *to* hitters and began throwing it *past* them.

Perhaps the single most important event in the history of pitching occurred in the 19th century when a young man named Candy Cummings discovered the curveball. For Candy, this epiphany was something akin to Newton's discovery of gravity. Cummings said, "I began to watch the flight of the ball and distinctly saw it curve. A surge of joy flooded over me that I will never forget."

Since the discovery of the curveball, the art of pitching has placed a premium on deception, trickery and intimidation. And the game has become much more interesting. Thank you, Candy.

Mental attitude and concentration
are the keys to pitching.
Ferguson Jenkins

A can-do mentality is a pitcher's best friend.
Nolan Ryan

Great pitchers don't allow
trivial things to upset them.
Roger Craig

On the mound, block out all distractions.
Don Drysdale

Hitting is timing. Pitching is upsetting timing.

Warren Spahn

Pitching

The first thing any pitcher has got
   to develop – the biggest single item in
   his whole stock and trade – is control.
Babe Ruth

The plate is 17 inches wide,
   but I'm only concerned with 5 inches –
   2½ on the one side and 2½ on the other.
   I never use the rest.
Warren Spahn

The wildest pitch is not necessarily the one
   that goes back to the screen.
   It can also be the one that
   goes right down the middle.
Sandy Koufax

A pitcher who hasn't control,
   hasn't anything.
Joe McCarthy

Control is what kept me
in the big leagues for twenty-two years.

Cy Young

Control does not mean throwing strikes
every time. It means throwing where
a particular hitter will not hit it.

Juan Marichal

Throw your pitch, not the batter's pitch.

Sal Maglie

To fool the hitter – there's the rub.

Moe Berg

The best pitch looks like a strike ...
but isn't.

Warren Spahn

Pitching is the art of instilling fear.

Sandy Koufax

One of the most valuable weapons in
a pitcher's command is the brushback pitch.

Bob Gibson

You've got to keep the ball away from the
sweet part of the bat. To do that, the pitcher
has to move the hitter off the plate.

Don Drysdale

A pitcher must go out to the mound
with the attitude that he is the boss.

Ferguson Jenkins

Would I throw at my mother?
Only if she was crowding the plate.

Early Wynn

It helps if the hitter thinks you're a little crazy.

Nolan Ryan

Babe Ruth is dead – throw strikes.

Baseball Adage

Throw strikes, change speeds, and work fast.

Ray Miller

Watch the batter's feet.

Sal Maglie

If a man can beat you, walk him.

Satchel Paige

Each umpire has a different strike zone.

Tommy John

Luck, as well as skill, decides a game.
The pitcher's job is to minimize
the elements of luck.

Moe Berg

Pitching is like hitting is like broadcasting.
You've got to be you.

Don Drysdale

The knuckleball is different
than anything else in baseball.

Phil Niekro

If you make a mistake away, it's a single.
If you make a mistake inside, it's a home run.

Tim McCarver

Nobody likes the ball low and away,
but that's where they'll get it from me.

Satchel Paige

Pitching is a lonely business.

Sandy Koufax

Pitch within yourself.

Tom Seaver

If you think long, you think wrong.

Jim Kaat

Every team carries nine or ten pitchers. That's always the wrong number. Either six is too many or twelve ain't enough.

Earl Weaver

My pitching philosophy is simple. You gotta keep the ball off the fat part of the bat.

Satchel Paige

The secret to my pitching success? Clean living and a fast outfield.

Lefty Gomez

12

Playing the Field

The father of modern baseball, Alexander Cartwright, gave simple advice to his pitchers: "Let him hit it, boys — you've got fielders behind you."

Pitching and hitting make headlines, but crisp fielding and savvy base running win ball games. Playing the field is an art. Consider the words of the following artists.

Baseball is a game of ability and mobility,
not a game of strength.

Tony Kubek

Fundamentals are the most valuable tools
a player can possess. Bunt the ball
into the ground. Hit the cutoff man.
Take the extra base.
Learn the fundamentals.

Dick Williams

Good fielding and pitching, without hitting,
or vice versa, is like Ben Franklin's
half pair of scissors – ineffectual.

Moe Berg

Hitting alone will not win ball games.

Branch Rickey

There has never been a good baseball team
that was not good defensively.

Dick Howser

I don't like fellows
who drive in two runs
and let in three.

Casey Stengel

For the steal to be worth anything,
the runner should be safe
about 75 percent of the time.

Earl Weaver

In stealing bases, it's as important to know
when not to go as it is to know when to go.

Maury Wills

Nobody ever won a pennant
without a star shortstop.

Leo Durocher

My advice to third basemen?
Get your glove down on the ground
and in position to field the ball.

Brooks Robinson

The catcher is the Cerberus of baseball.

Moe Berg

Catching is the most demanding and
underrated job in sports.

Tim McCarver

Catchers are always in short supply.

Bill Veeck

You'll never see two ball games alike,
   never two plays alike.

Harry Caray

Players who commit errors need
   reassurance from the pitcher,
   who must harbor no grudges.

Roger Craig

Positioning the defense
   can be worth five or ten games a year.

Whitey Herzog

An outfielder who throws behind a runner
is locking the barn door
after the horse is stolen.

Joe McCarthy

The phrase "off with the crack of the bat,"
while romantic, is really meaningless,
since the outfielder should be in motion
long before he hears the sound
of the ball meeting the bat.

Joe DiMaggio

Catching a fly ball is a pleasure,
but knowing what to do with it
after you catch it is a business.

Tommy Henrich

Playing without
the fundamentals
is like eating without
a knife and fork.
You make a mess.

Dick Williams

13

Managing

After his Bronx Bombers won the 1958 World Series, Casey Stengel was mobbed by reporters. In a moment of unbridled joy, Casey spoke for managers everywhere when he observed, "I couldn't have done it without my players."

Casey understood a cardinal truth : Good players need good managers ... and vice versa.

A manager who is not in sole charge
of his players cannot run his team.

Branch Rickey

I don't have any privileged characters
on my ball clubs.

John McGraw

Here's what I know about managing
a baseball team: If you get good players,
and they play well, you're a genius.

Whitey Herzog

The secret of managing a club is to keep
the five guys who hate you away from
the five who are undecided.

Casey Stengel

Baseball is a simple game.
>   If you have good players and keep
>   them in the right frame of mind,
>   then the manager is a success.

Sparky Anderson

A manager of a team is like a stagecoach.
>   He can't move unless he has the horses.

Pete Rose

Managers don't win games.
>   They prepare players to win games.

Dick Williams

A manager doesn't do much that's brilliant.
>   Mostly, it's our job to make sure we
>   don't lose games unnecessarily.

Earl Weaver

Managing is like holding a dove in your hand.
>   Squeeze too hard and you kill it,
>   not hard enough and it flies away.

Tommy Lasorda

Be satisfied with players who have
one or two skills and make the most of them.
Not everybody can be Mickey Mantle.

Earl Weaver

Managing is like playing bridge.
You've got strategy and bluffing and finesse,
but in the end you better have more
trump cards than the other guy.

Whitey Herzog

A manager has the cards dealt him,
and he must play them, like it or not.
Play your strongest hand.

Miller Huggins

Most managers think winning
creates chemistry. I think chemistry
creates winning.

Sparky Anderson

The most important part of managing? Be yourself.

Walter Alston

You always have to believe in yourself
before others can believe in you.

Tommy Lasorda

Playing and managing both revolve around
a single basic concept – common sense.

Earl Weaver

The fewer rules you've got,
the better the chances they'll be obeyed.

Whitey Herzog

Once a manager gets good players, about 75 percent of his job is handling the pitching.

Whitey Herzog

You need two things to be a good manager: a sense of humor and a good bull pen.

Whitey Herzog

Play for one run, lose by one run.

Earl Weaver

Managing is getting paid for home runs someone else hits.

Casey Stengel

14

Winning and Losing

By losing 116 games in 1916, the Philadelphia Athletics set a standard for futility. After the final game of the season, Manager Connie Mack was asked for his reaction. Mack paused for a moment, then responded, "You can't win 'em all."

A generation later, Casey Stengel managed an equally inept squad, the New York Mets. Casey asked fans to "Come and see my amazin' Mets. I've been in the game a hundred years, but I now see new ways to lose that I never knew existed before."

Both Stengel and Mack understood that even if you lose the game, you should never lose your sense of humor.

There is no known substitute for winning,
and no known cure for losing.

Bill Veeck

The only thing that really satisfies and
makes you happy in this game is
the end product – winning.

Earl Weaver

Winning 20 games doesn't begin
to compare with winning the pennant.

Bob Gibson

The main idea is to win.

John McGraw

Baseball is disguised combat.
Baseball is violence under wraps.

Willie Mays

Baseball is something like a war.

Ty Cobb

Baseball is war!

A. G. Spalding

Most one-run games are lost, not won.

Gene Mauch

I don't mind being beaten, but I hate to lose.

Reggie Jackson

You gotta lose 'em some time.
When you do, lose 'em right.

Casey Stengel

You can learn a
little from victory.
You can learn
everything from defeat.

Christy Mathewson

Unless the whole organization is working
together for one common purpose,
the club doesn't win, and
the manager gets fired.

Whitey Herzog

To make a ball club a champion,
the effort has to start with the bat boy
and move right up to the owner.

Brooks Robinson

The winning "we" attitude starts
at the top of the organization.

Pete Rose

The best organization wins.

Babe Ruth

Perhaps the truest axiom is
    that the toughest thing to do is repeat.
        The tendency is to relax
        without even knowing it.

Walter Alston

You're never as good as you look
    when you're winning, and you're never
    as bad as you look when you're losing.

Earl Weaver

Never give the other guy the satisfaction
    of hearing you squawk.

Ty Cobb

It's takes pitching, hitting and defense.
    Any two can win.
    All three make you unbeatable.

Joe Garagiola

Good pitching will always stop good hitting and vice versa.

Casey Stengel

15

Observations on Baseball, X-Rays, Slumps and Other Mysteries

We conclude with an assortment of thoughts on an assortment of topics. Enjoy.

Why buy good luggage?
You only use it when you travel.

Yogi Berra

If you don't go to their funeral,
they won't go to yours.

Yogi Berra

If people don't want to come out to the park,
nobody's going to stop them.

Yogi Berra

You can observe a lot just by watching.

Yogi Berra

I don't want to make the wrong mistake.

Yogi Berra

Little League is great because
it keeps parents off the streets.

Yogi Berra

I really didn't say half the things I've said.

Yogi Berra

Baseball is not the player's game or
the manager's game. It's not the owner's
game. It's the fan's game.

Sparky Anderson

Ball parks should be happy places.
They should always smell like fresh-cut grass.

Bill Veeck

To receive an ovation in a baseball uniform
is the greatest feeling in the world.

Pete Rose

Always give an autograph
when somebody asks you.

Tommy Lasorda

A player ought to spend 20 minutes
of his time each day signing autographs
and meeting fans.

Ferguson Jenkins

Any ballplayer who don't sign autographs
for little kids ain't American.

Rogers Hornsby

Don't worry about your individual numbers.
Worry about the team. If the team
is successful, each of you
will be successful, too.

Branch Rickey

In baseball, the individual is highlighted,
but in the end, his performance
means nothing outside the team.

Bob Costas

In baseball, you're almost totally dependent
on your teammates.

Bob Gibson

Baseball always has been and always will be
a game demanding team play.

Babe Ruth

What comes first is the team.

Pete Rose

Associate with those
who help you believe in yourself.

Brooks Robinson

The doctors X-rayed my head and found nothing.

Dizzy Dean

I went through life as the player
to be named later.

Joe Garagiola

It's hard to be lucky
when your pitching is bad.

Walter Alston

The best possible thing in baseball
is winning the World Series. The second best
thing is losing the World Series.

Tommy Lasorda

People complain about the weather.
Any weather is good as long
as you're around to feel it.

Branch Rickey

It ain't braggin' if you can do it.

Dizzy Dean

Comparisons with other people
are like weeds. As soon as you deal with one,
another one pops up.

Hank Aaron

Uniforms change, but friendships don't.

Whitey Herzog

Old-timer's games are great.
It's wonderful meeting so many old friends
that I didn't used to like.

Casey Stengel

The fastball is the only pitch
that can't be taught. You have it,
or you don't.

Juan Marichal

Slumps are like a soft bed. They're easy
to get into and hard to get out of.

Johnny Bench

I made up my mind, but I made it up
both ways.

Casey Stengel

There is one word in America that
says it all and that word is
"You never know."

Joaquin Andujar

If you'd like to do something really great,
be an organ donor.

Mickey Mantle

History gives us hope because it shows
how quickly some things can change.

Monte Irvin

The real riches of this game are in the thrills, not in the money.

Ernie Banks

Baseball is still the greatest game.

Mickey Mantle

I thank heaven we have baseball in this world.

Babe Ruth

Baseball stays with you.

Stan Musial

I'd like to finish it by saying to all you kids: Take good care of yourself and go out there and make us proud of you.

Mickey Mantle

Sources

Hank Aaron 33, 38, 62, 152
Joe Adcock 89
Walter Alston 28, 62, 64, 66, 131, 141, 151
Sparky Anderson 129, 130, 146
Joaquin Andujar 153
Luke Appling 47
Ernie Banks 22, 26, 72, 155
Johnny Bench 153
Chief Bender 28
Moe Berg 111, 115, 120, 123
Yogi Berra 25, 34, 41, 43, 57, 61, 68, 102, 144,
    145
Ping Bodie 78
Ken Boyer 82
Ralph Branca 93
Lou Brock 48, 64, 90
Dr. Bobby Brown 100
Roy Campanella 72, 87
Harry Caray 38, 62, 124
Alexander Cartwright 119
Rico Carty 42
Happy Chandler 86
Roberto Clemente 90
Ty Cobb 46, 53, 54, 71, 83, 97, 98, 104, 137, 141
Rocky Colavito 43
Chuck Conners 54

Bob Costas 84, 148
Roger Craig 108, 124
Candy Cummings 107
Dizzy Dean 52, 150, 152
Joe DiMaggio 88, 94, 125
Larry Doby 86
Don Drysdale 42, 89, 108, 113, 115
Leo Durocher 122
Charles H. Ebbets 16
Bob Feller 36, 83
Charlie Finley 17, 70
Curt Flood 88
Joe Garagiola 47, 82, 141, 151
Lou Gehrig 46, 92
Cesar Geronimo 59
Bob Gibson 33, 113, 136, 148
Josh Gibson 81
Lefty Gomez 118
Harvey Haddix 94
Ernie Harwell 18
Tommy Henrich 125
Whitey Herzog 26, 124, 128, 130, 132, 133, 140,
     152
Russ Hodges 93
Herbert Hoover 17
Rogers Hornsby 100, 104, 147

Dick Howser 120
Waite Hoyt 78
Carl Hubbell 71
Miller Huggins 130
Monte Irvin 45, 154
Reggie Jackson 53, 138
Ferguson Jenkins 55, 108, 113, 147
Tommy John 19, 45, 61, 62, 74, 114
Carl Jung 77
Jim Kaat 116
Wee Willie Keeler 103
Sandy Koufax 45, 110, 112, 116
Tony Kubek 47, 120
Judge Kenesaw Mountain Landis 17, 35
Don Larson 96
Tommy Lasorda 20, 21, 44, 70, 73, 129, 132,
     147, 151
Charlie Lau 98, 99
Vernon Law 31, 60, 71
Bob Lemon 72
Henry Wadsworth Longfellow 16
Connie Mack 16, 21, 135
Sal Maglie 111, 114
Mickey Mantle 19, 32, 33, 37, 51, 52, 61, 83, 84,
     85, 89, 92, 94, 154, 155, 156
Juan Marichal 111, 153

Roger Maris 24
Christy Mathewson 24, 44, 139
Gene Mauch 138
Willie Mays 27, 74, 85, 137
Bill Mazeroski 48
Joe McCarthy 24, 30, 54, 65, 70, 75, 81, 92,
    110, 125
Tim McCarver 48, 66, 82, 85, 115, 123
John McGraw 64, 80, 128, 136
Tug McGraw 46
Ray Miller 114
Johnny Mize 101
Stan Musial 28, 97, 98, 106, 155
Phil Niekro 115
Sadaharu Oh 38, 41, 53
Buck O'Neil 19, 66, 88
Satchel Paige 25, 29, 40, 57, 114, 115, 117
Herb Pennock 30
Grantland Rice 45, 75, 78, 80
Branch Rickey 19, 24, 44, 47, 53, 55, 57, 58, 64,
    71, 75, 77, 80, 82, 86, 102, 120, 128, 148, 151
Robin Roberts 46
Bill "Bojangles" Robinson 87
Brooks Robinson
    15, 18, 25, 50, 123, 140, 149
Frank Robinson 62

Jackie Robinson 39, 87

Preacher Roe 61

Pete Rose 15, 32, 36, 52, 54, 75, 90, 101, 102,
    105, 129, 140, 146, 149

Babe Ruth 16, 25, 30, 31, 49, 52, 76, 79, 100,
    110, 140, 149, 155

Nolan Ryan 44, 108, 113

Vin Scully 40

Tom Seaver 116

George Sisler 79

Duke Snider 87, 99

Red Smith 17, 86

Warren Spahn 81, 109, 110, 111

A. G. Spalding 16, 70, 137

Tris Speaker 32

Willie Stargell 26

Casey Stengel 28, 32, 40, 41, 63, 88, 89, 121,
    127, 128, 134, 135, 138, 142, 152, 153

Billy Sunday 74

Bobby Thomson 93

Pie Traynor 90

Manny Trillo 67

Bill Veeck 18, 20, 21, 55, 56, 123, 136, 146

Honus Wagner 81

Earl Weaver 20, 31, 72, 90, 116, 122, 129, 130,
    132, 133, 136, 141

Wes Westrum 21
Walt Whitman 17
Dick Williams 120, 126, 129
Ted Williams 36, 52, 74, 79, 89, 99, 100, 101
Maury Wills 122
Early Wynn 113
Cy Young 111

About the Author

Criswell Freeman is a Doctor of Clinical Psychology living in Nashville, Tennessee. He is the author of *When Life Throws You a Curveball, Hit It* and *The Wisdom Series* from Walnut Grove Press. He is also a published country music songwriter. His promising baseball career ended prematurely when it was discovered that he couldn't hit the curveball.

About Wisdom Books

Wisdom Books chronicle memorable quotations in an easy-to-read style. Written by Criswell Freeman, this series provides inspiring, thoughtful and humorous messages from entertainers, athletes, scientists, politicians, clerics, writers and renegades. Each title focuses on a particular region or special interest.

Combining his passion for quotations with extensive training in psychology, Dr. Freeman revisits timeless themes such as perseverance, courage, love, forgiveness and faith.

"Quotations help us remember the simple yet profound truths that give life perspective and meaning," notes Freeman. "When it comes to life's most important lessons, we can all use gentle reminders."

The Wisdom Series
by Dr. Criswell Freeman

Wisdom Made In America
ISBN 1-887655-07-7

The Book of Southern Wisdom
ISBN 0-9640955-3-X

The Book of Country Music Wisdom
ISBN 0-9640955-1-3

The Golfer's Book of Wisdom
ISBN 0-9640955-6-4

The Wisdom of Southern Football
ISBN 0-9640955-7-2

The Book of Texas Wisdom
ISBN 0-9640955-8-0

The Book of Florida Wisdom
ISBN 0-9640955-9-9

The Book of Stock Car Wisdom
ISBN 1-887655-12-3

The Wisdom of Old-Time Baseball
ISBN 1-887655-08-5

Wisdom Books are available through
booksellers everywhere. For information about
a retailer near you, call 1-800-256-8584.